SCILLY'S WILDLIFE HERITAGE

Adrian Spalding and Pat Sargeant

GW00602017

INTRODUCTION

This book is the first general but comprehensive account of the fauna and flora of Scilly. The Isles of Scilly have a unique though impoverished wildlife, linked to the main habitats of maritime heath and grassland, gorse and bracken scrub, sand dunes, shingle beaches, wetlands and wooded areas. Scilly is well known for rare migrant birds and increasingly for rare migrant moths and dragonflies, but the islands are also home to species found nowhere else in Britain, as well as many species that can only survive in the generally warm frost-free maritime environment of the extreme western parts of the British Isles. There is no doubt that the wildlife of Scilly, along with its stunning scenery, helps contribute to the unique character that makes these islands such an exciting place to live and visit and so valuable a biodiversity resource that the archipelago has been declared a Special Area of Conservation.

Aerial view of the Isles of Scilly

THE IMPORTANCE OF THE ISLES OF SCILLY FOR WILDLIFE

The wildlife of Scilly depends on a variety of factors. Perhaps the most important factor is the position of the islands surrounded by sea in the extreme south west of Britain, with warm winters, cool summers and exposure to the influence of the prevailing westerly winds. Species can survive here which could not tolerate the cold winters of the mainland; on the other hand, thermophilic (warmth-loving) species are absent because the summers are too cool. Species diversity is generally low, both because of the small area of land and its isolation from the mainland. Nevertheless, the islands contain no less than 78 nationally rare terrestrial plants and animals. Some of these species are accidental imports that came with exotic plants from the Southern Hemisphere. The importance of the archipelago for wildlife is emphasised by the fact that 14 species found in Britain since 1950 occur only in Scilly.

Terrestrial Red Data Book plants and animals recorded in Scilly since 1950

GROUP	TOTAL NUMBER
Bats	1
Beetles	5
Birds	28
Bugs	2
Lichens	14
Liverworts	8
Mammals	1
Mosses	4
Moths	2
Spiders	1
Vascular plants	12
TOTAL	**78**

Examples of species found within Britain only in Scilly since 1950

Achaearanea veruculata	a spider
Buellia abstracta	a lichen
Catillaria subviridis	a lichen
Clitarchus hookeri	Smooth Stick-insect
Crocidura suaveolens	Scilly Shrew
Heterodermia propagulifera	Coralloid Rosette-lichen
Oinophila v-flava	Yellow V moth
Ophioglossumm lusitanicum	Least Adder's Tongue
Ornithopus pinnatus	Orange Bird's-foot
Piesma quadratum spergulariae	Beet Leaf Bug
Sematophyllum substrumulosum	a moss
Telaranea murphyae	a liverwort
Usnea subscabrosa	a lichen
Viola kitailbeliana	Dwarf Pansy

THE POST-GLACIAL ENVIRONMENT AND WILDLIFE

Around 18,000 years ago, during the coldest part of the Ice Age when the sea level was approximately 130 metres lower than today, Scilly was part of the British mainland. Most of Scilly, together with Cornwall and southern England, was free of ice, but the soil would have been frozen and have supported only tundra vegetation. By the beginning of the post-glacial period the sea level in the south west of England had risen considerably to approximately 35-40 metres below that of today, with the result that the land bridge to Scilly was flooded. At that time (around 10,000BC), Scilly may have consisted of one large island. As the ice sheets melted, continued sea level rises lead to the submergence of low-lying land and the creation (by 3000BC) of a number of separate islands – the main one encompassing St Mary's, Bryher, Tresco and St Martin's, with St Agnes, Annet and Western Rocks forming three smaller tracts of land. It may not have been until the end of the Roman period that today's islands began to appear.

Some of the insects present on Scilly reflect the post-glacial sequence of colonisation. The Field Grasshopper, Grey Bush-cricket, Great Green Bush-cricket, Lesser Cockroach, Red-barbed Ant and Common Blue butterfly are possibly very early post-glacial colonists, reaching Scilly before it was cut-off from the mainland. Those species that have developed unique subspecies or races (such as the Scilly Bee, Beet Leaf Bug, Meadow Brown butterfly) have probably been on Scilly for many hundreds of years.

THE ARRIVAL OF PEOPLE

Pollen evidence from peat deposits (e.g. under parts of Higher Moors on St Mary's) indicates that by about 5000BC Scilly was covered in mixed oak woodland, comprised of Oak, Hazel, Elm and Ash, with Birch in exposed coastal locations. There is evidence for semi-nomadic hunter-gatherers living here at this time, and from around 3000BC people began clearing the woodland for farming. Arable crops and domestic animals were introduced from the mainland. Bones of Horse have

been found on St Mary's dating from the 2nd to 7th centuries AD and Ox probably occurred on St Mary's between 1700 and 1000BC. By the end of the prehistoric period the islands had become transformed into an open landscape similar to that of today – cultivated fields, pasture and heathland, fringed by coastal dunes. As trade with mainland Europe as well as with Cornwall began, animals and plants were introduced to the islands.

It has been suggested that mammals such as Pallas' Vole, Roe Deer and Red Deer arrived on the islands across the land bridge before it was flooded. Bones of Roe and Red Deer dating from the Bronze Age have been found on St Mary's and other islands. However, it is more likely that deer were brought over in boats for food and skins. This is supported by the fact that many other wild mammals found on the mainland (e.g. as foxes, badgers, stoats and weasels) have never been recorded on Scilly. Pallas' Vole, Wood Mouse and Scilly Shrew also probably arrived this way. Many plants were probably also accidental imports, e.g. Orange Bird's-foot, Dwarf Pansy and Least Adder's Tongue may have been brought here from southern France, Portugal and Spain.

HUMAN INTRODUCTION OF WILDLIFE

The Elder tree was introduced to Scilly by the monks of Tavistock sometime after 1120 and became the dominant tree on Tresco, which was formerly known as Innischawe (island of the Elder

Hedgehog in a garden

trees). The rabbit reached Scilly before 1176 (the first record of Rabbits in Britain), and were probably farmed. The House Cricket certainly reached Scilly before 1900. Some Red-legged Partridge were put out on St Martin's and Tresco in the 1850s (they had died out by 1864). The flightless Common Cockroach has also been recorded on Scilly, certainly arriving by ship. More recently, the Long-winged Cone-head reached Scilly in 1989, probably flying from the Channel Islands. Many species have arrived on imported plants, such as the New Zealand Land-hopper *Arcitalitrus dorrieni* (first discovered in 1925), the Prickly Stick-insect and the Smooth Stick-insect (arriving from New Zealand some time prior to 1949), the New Zealand Flatworm (first found on Tresco in 1960), the spider *Achaearanea veruculata* (arriving from New Zealand or Australia before 1974 when it was recorded on Tresco), the moss *Eriopus apiculatus* (known on Tresco since 1967) and the liverwort

Telaranea murphyae (known in Britain only from Tresco). The red seaweed *Pikea californica* probably arrived from its home in the Pacific on the floats of flying boats during the Second World War. Recent deliberate introductions (with varied success) include attempts to start colonies of the European Tree Frog, Budgerigar, Bobwhite Quail, Golden Pheasant and Hedgehog. Not all species arriving on the islands find conditions to their liking, and many do not settle. For example, Short-eared Owls are occasional visitors in the winter but do not breed, perhaps because of the lack of Field Voles. Other species may have died out. For example, what may be the remains of a Chough have been found on St Martin's dating from sometime between the 2nd and 7th century AD. The Chough is not known to have nested recently, although two were shot here at the turn of the century.

Ramalina lichen on coastal rocks

MOSSES AND LIVERWORTS

Several rare mosses have been found on Scilly. *Sematophyllum substrumulosum* is known in Britain only from St Mary's and Tresco where it was discovered in 1995. It generally grows on the old bark of Monterey Pine trees. It may be a natural colonist here, or it may have been introduced accidentally with horticultural plants. Elsewhere, it has been recorded from the Azores, the Canary Islands, Madeira and parts of Europe.

Rare liverworts include *Telaranea murphyae*, which was probably introduced to Tresco from the Southern Hemisphere. Two other southern hemisphere species, *Lophocolea bispinosa* and *Lophocolea semiteres*, have a strange distribution in Britain, being found only in Scotland and Scilly, and were probably introduced on exotic trees.

LICHENS

Scilly's pollution-free oceanic climate has encouraged the development of a particularly rich and diverse lichen flora with over 250 species recorded. Scilly supports the only European record of the Coralloid Rosette-lichen *Heterodermia propagulifera*, which grows on the lichen-rich heathland on Castle Down, Tresco. The Golden Hair-lichen *Teloschistes flavicans* is chiefly found on short turf, heathland and rocky outcrops immediately adjacent to the sea. This lichen requires a pollution-free oceanic climate hence its main distribution in Britain is limited to Scilly and south west England. The Lungwort Lichens *Lobaria pulmonaria* and *Lobaria scrobiculata* normally grow on trees, but in Scilly occur on the heathland habitats of Tresco.

VASCULAR PLANTS

The Isles of Scilly are especially important for a range of plant species which thrive in the maritime conditions here. These plants make up the main habitats of maritime grassland and heathland, wetland, hedge and shelter belt, sand dune, sea cliff, and bulb and arable field. The wild places are dominated by Gorse (both European and Western), Bramble, Bracken and Heather (both Ling

Agapanthus

and Bell Heather), with areas of maritime and dune grassland kept short by a combination of the wind and rabbits. On many islands (such as in Great Bay on St Martin's) one can follow the natural succesion of vegetation from strandline vegetation on the shore through dune grassland through heathland to Gorse and Bramble scrub on top of the hill. Some of the commonest plants are Bramble, Common Bird's-foot-trefoil, European Gorse, Ling, Red Fescue, Thrift, Tormentil, Western Gorse, Wood Sage and Yorkshire Fog. Unfortunately, in places the more fragile habitats (such as dune grassland) are beginning to scrub over, a consequence of the cessation of grazing and the reduction in rabbit populations following myxomatosis. However, several national rarities occur, and Scilly is probably one of the best places to see plants such as Early Meadow-grass and Smaller Tree-mallow. Many introduced species occur, especially on the hedgebanks where *Pittosporum crassifolium* is common and has become naturalised in places. Other aliens and escapes (some unwelcome) include Apple-of-Peru (on cultivated

Golden Hair-lichen

land), Bermuda Buttercup (along roadside verges), German Ivy (on hedgebanks), Hottentot Fig (common on cliffs), New Zealand Flax (on cliffs), Rosy Garlic (roadside verges) and Spring Starflower (roadside verges). Plants of arable fields include Corn Marigold, Corn Spurrey, Fumitory, Hairy Buttercup, Long-headed Poppy, the introduced Rough-fruited Buttercup, Small-flowered Buttercup and Small-flowered Catchfly, as well as a lovely blue form of Scarlet Pimpernel. Elm trees are still relatively common on Scilly, together with Elder; Oak is rare.

Nationally rare plants which can be found on Scilly

Aeonium

NAME	HABITAT
Babington's Leek	Dune grassland
Balm-leaved Figwort	Dune grassland
Dwarf Pansy	Dune grassland
Early Meadow-grass	Maritime grassland
Four-leaved Allseed	Bulb and arable fields
Least Adder's-tongue	Maritime grassland and heathland
Orange Bird's-foot	Maritime grassland and heathland
Purple Ramping Fumitory	Bulb and arable fields
Shore Dock	Beaches
Small Adder's-tongue	Maritime grassland and heathland
Smaller Tree-mallow	Dune grassland, bulb and arable fields
Western Clover	Maritime grassland
Western Fumitory	Bulb and arable fields, hedgebanks

Alien plants and garden escapes on Scilly

NAME	COUNTRY OF ORIGIN
Aeonium	Canary Isles
Agapanthus	South Africa
Apple-of-Peru	Peru
Arum Lily	South Africa
Bear's-breech	Mediterranean region
Belladonna Lily	South Africa
Bermuda Buttercup	South Africa
Evening Primrose	North America
German Ivy	South Africa
Hottentot Fig	South Africa
Japanese Knotweed	Japan
Lewis's Hebe	New Zealand
Libertia	Chile
Monkey Flower	North America
Montbretia	-
New Zealand Flax	New Zealand
Pigweed	North America
Pittosporum	New Zealand
Red Valerian	Mediterranean region
Rosy Garlic	Mediterranean region
Rough-fruited Buttercup	Southern Europe
Spring Beauty	North America

Spring Beauty

Spring Snowflake	Mediterranean region
Spring Starflower	South America
Tamarisk	Mediterranean region
Thorn Apple	America
Tree Echium	Canary Isles
Tree Lupin	California
Watsonia	South Africa
Whistling Jacks	Mediterranean region

Babington's Leek *Allium ampeloprasum* var. *babingtonii*

Babington's Leek was first discovered on the Lizard in west Cornwall and its distribution is confined to western Ireland and south west Britain. This rare variety of Wild Leek is a spectacular plant often growing to a height of over 2m. It is a tall stout perennial with white to purple flowers, growing extensively across Scilly, especially on the stable back-dune areas. It is often found on waste ground or old rubbish tips. Particularly prominent plants can be seen growing behind Lower Town Bay on St Martin's.

Balm-leaved Figwort *Scrophularia scorodonia*

This nationally rare figwort, often reaching 1m in height, is widespread throughout Scilly but is especially abundant in stable dune habitats, where it often grows in association with Marram and Bramble. It has a square, but unwinged, stem with toothed hairy downy leaves, from which it derives its name. The flowers are unspectacular, dull brown-purple with broad membranous margins. The larvae of the nationally rare moth *Nothris congressariella* feed on Balm-leaved Figwort.

Babington's Leek   Beth Tonkin

Babington's Leek   Beth Tonkin

Dwarf Pansy

Dwarf Pansy *Viola kitaibeliana*

In Britain the Dwarf Pansy is restricted to the Channel Isles and the Isles of Scilly, where it has declined significantly since it was first noted on Tresco in 1873; it is now restricted to Tean and Bryher. It is a very small plant, normally only some 4-8mm in height, with cream flowers often with a yellow or pale-violet centre. It grows as an annual in short grazed turf on sandy habitats behind dunes, often associated with disturbed ground around rabbit holes or adjacent to small quarries. It flowers early, any time from March onwards, then dries up and disappears, sometimes as soon as May. The largest colony occurs on a sandy dune-grassland immediately behind the coastal dunes at Rushy Bay on Bryher, with a total population of about 2,000. The population was gradually declining with increased disturbance, fewer rabbits and an increase in competing vegetation (especially Bracken and Gorse) until the great storms of the 1989/1990 winter when the sea breached the dunes at Rushy Bay. Following the inundation by the sea, the sand plain was colonised by giant Dwarf Pansies (some 5cm wide and over 2cm high), leading to a peak population in 1992 of about 20,000 plants. How-

ever, by 1993 Sand Sedge and Red Fescue were forming a dense turf and the numbers of Dwarf Pansy were returning to normal - that is, until the next great storm.

Least Adder's-tongue *Ophioglossum lusitanicum*

This is the smallest and rarest species of Adder's-tongue Fern in Britain. Outside mainland Europe it only occurs on the Channel Isles and St Agnes, where it grows in areas of short turf on shallow soils on the south side of the island. It is a tiny green non-flowering fern, normally found above ground only between November and April, and is rarely seen by visitors. It was first discovered by chance on St Agnes when John Raven, a botanist on holiday in Scilly in March 1950, was having a picnic on Wingletang. It can only survive if the heathland is managed (e.g. by rough grazing) and the risk of damaging accidental fires kept to a minimum.

Orange Bird's-foot *Ornithopus pinnatus*

This rare Bird's-foot has characteristic 6-8mm long tiny orange-yellow flowers occurring as either solitary flowers or in heads of 2-5. The low prostrate slender plant is a hairless (or almost hairless) perennial confined to short maritime or heathy turf, although sometimes occurring on disturbed sandy soil in arable fields or adjacent to sand quarries. In Scilly, it has been found on several islands, although recently on St Mary's it has only been seen as a garden plant.

Pat Sargeant monitoring the Dwarf Pansy

Orange Bird's-foot

Shore Dock *Rumex rupestris*

The Shore Dock is the rarest species of dock in Europe and is one of the botanical highlights of Scilly. In Britain the plant is mainly restricted to coastal locations in south west England (also Wales). Scilly contains about 50% of the British population, although the plant only occurs on a small number of islands with no more than 50 plants at any one site.

Shore Dock grows along the coastal margin, from the strand line to wave cut platforms, raised beaches and low cliffs, often associated with wet flushes and seepages. Unfortunately, these locations are often affected by coastal protection works, recreational pressures and storm damage. There is some evidence of recent loss due to plants being used to start beach bonfires.

Western Ramping-fumitory *Fumaria occidentalis*

Western Ramping-fumitory is an endemic species only found in Scilly and Cornwall, with its stronghold on St Mary's where it occurs on stone walls, hedges, arable fields and gardens. This species is often associated with human activity and disturbance, and was once widespread throughout the bulb fields. Recently, however, changing agricultural practices on Scilly have dramatically reduced its distribution. The flowers are white at first, turning bright pink with a dark purple apex. The tiny 3mm fruit are notched at the tip.

Shore Dock

Western Ramping-fumitory
Hazel Meredith

INVERTEBRATES OTHER THAN INSECTS

Of the many invertebrates occurring in Scilly, several stand out because of their rarity in Britain or because of their origins in the Southern Hemisphere. For example, the New Zealand Land-hopper *Arcitalitrus dorrieni* was first discovered as new to science on Tresco in 1925 despite being a native of New Zealand. It lives in dead leaves and damp humus, where it might be mistaken for a tiny brown shrimp. The spider *Achaearanea veruculata* has its sole European distribution on Scilly, where it has been recorded on Tresco. Two flatworms have been recorded, both aliens from the southern hemisphere (probably imported in soil on garden plants). *Geoplana sanguinea* (from Australia and New Zealand) was first found in Tresco in 1960 and has since been found in many parts of Britain including Northern Ireland. *Geoplana coxii* (from New Zealand) was also first found in Britain in Tresco and has since been found in Cornwall. Both species eat earthworms and can be garden pests. Several troglophiles (species adapted to life in caves) have been found in Piper's Hole on Tresco, using Danish Blue cheese as an attractant. These species include some white springtails and a small leafhopper *Balclutha saltuella*, both new to Britain. It is possible that there could be several other species in other caves which will be new to Britain.

Pat Sargeant in Piper's Hole
Beth Tonkin

Bulb fields

GRASSHOPPERS, CRICKETS AND ALLIED INSECTS

The Field Grasshopper can be found on St Agnes, Gugh, St Mary's, Samson, Bryher, Tresco (including Skirt Island), St Helen's, Tean and St Martin's. The Desert Locust is an occasional visitor to the islands and the spectacular Blue-winged Grasshopper was recorded as a stray on St Mary's in 1903. The only bush-crickets are the Grey Bush-cricket, Great Green Bush-cricket (both probably early post-glacial colonists), Speckled Bush-cricket, Short-winged Cone-head (first recorded on St Agnes in 1990) and Long-winged Cone-head (first recorded in 1989). The House-cricket was generally common in the 19th century but probably died out because of the concentrated use of dieldrin and aldrin on the bulb fields, before being refound on St Mary's in 1992 on a rubbish tip.

Other species include the Common Groundhopper (on Tresco), the native Lesser Cockroach, the ubiquitous Common Earwig and the nationally local Lesnei's Earwig. Two species of stick-insect are found on Scilly. The Prickly Stick-insect has been recorded in the Abbey Gardens and New Grimsby on Tresco, to which it was introduced on plants from New Zealand early this century. It feeds on Bramble and garden plants such as Pittosporum and Fuchsia. The many spines on its body (especially the head and thorax) immediately distinguish it from the Smooth Stick-insect.

Field Grasshopper

Grey bush-cricket   Chris Haes

Desert Locust   Chris Haes

Golden-ringed Dragonfly

The Smooth Stick-insect *Clitarchus hookeri*

The Smooth Stick-insect has only been recorded in Britain from the Abbey Gardens on Tresco. It was first found in 1949 but probably came here at the same time as the Prickly Stick-insect (about 1907) and remained unnoticed. Smooth Stick-insects are usually green, sometimes brown, with a black line on the thorax, up to 6cm long. Only females have been found on Tresco, where they reproduce by parthenogenesis, females laying unfertilised eggs which develop into females. The adults die during the winter, when the eggs survive the cold, wet weather. They have been recorded feeding on Bramble and garden plants such as *Leptospermum*. The best time to observe them is at night.

DRAGONFLIES AND DAMSELFLIES

There is very little freshwater in Scilly so it is not surprising that only 2 species of dragonfly are long-term residents here, the Common Blue-tailed Damselfly *Ischnura elegans* and the Common Darter *Sympetrum striolatum*. However, 9 other species have been recorded, out of about 39 resident species in Britain. The best place to watch dragonflies is probably the Great Pool on Tresco.

Dragonflies on Scilly

SPECIES NAME	ST MARY'S	TRESCO	ST AGNES
Common Blue Damsell	●		
Common Blue-tailed Damselfly	●	●	●
Common Darter	●	●	●
Common Hawker		●	●
Emperor Dragonfly	●		
Golden-ringed Dragonfly		●	
Green-winged Darner			●
Migrant Hawker	●		●
Red-veined Darter		●	
Southern Hawker	●		●
Sympetrum flaveolum	●		

Prickly stick-insect   Chris Haes

BUGS (HEMIPTERA)

About 46 bugs have been recorded on Scilly since 1900, compared with about 500 on mainland Britain. Species found include the nationally rare ground-bug *Emblethis griseus* and the nationally local Spurgebug *Dicranocephalus agilis*. The Beet Leaf Bug *Piesma quadratum* has a subspecies unique to Scilly - ssp *spergulariae*. It feeds on Rock Sea-spurrey and the adults have been found on the cliffs and headlands of St Mary's, St Martins, St Agnes, Bryher and Samson where the foodplant grows.

Trioza vitrioradiata

This jumping plant louse is a pest species from New Zealand and feeds on *Pittosporum*. First found in Britain at St Mawes in Cornwall in 1993, it has since been discovered in Scilly on all the main islands, even on hedges surrounding abandoned bulb fields on Gugh. Its range in Britain is limited by the distribution of its foodplant, which is frost sensitive. The larvae feed on the young leaves, which react by forming light green pits in conspicuous infestations which make the foliage unsuitable for sale. The larvae may be moved around Scilly by the transport of foliage, although the adults probably reached Gugh by being carried on the wind.

BEETLES

About 380 species of beetle have been recorded on the Isles of Scilly, out of a total mainland population of around 4,000. The Rose Chafer is especially widespread in Scilly, having been recorded on seven islands. The adult beetles are fond of the sun and can often be found resting on Thrift and other flowers. A rare dark form *ab nigra* can occasionally be seen. The male of the Minotaur Beetle is most distinctive with three horns on its thorax; it can be found in sandy places where the adults and larvae feed on rabbit dung. It is interesting to speculate what it fed on before rabbits arrived on the islands - or did it arrive on Scilly with (or after) the rabbits themselves? The nationally rare Henbane Flea Beetle is associated with Henbane, which has been found in waste places on a number of islands. Being poisonous, Henbane is often deliberately destroyed, with the result that the beetle (recorded only in 1836 and 1931) may now be extinct here.

ANTS AND BEES

Red-barbed Ant Formica rufibarbis

There are 11 species of ant recorded on Scilly, compared with about 36 species on the mainland. The nationally rare Red-barbed Ant is found in Britain only in Surrey and on Scilly. It lives beneath stones on uncultivated heathland. It probably existed on Scilly before people arrived, unlike another ant *Formica fusca* (a more recent arrival), which might be displacing it here. It has a high sunlight requirement and colonies are particularly threatened by the spread of bracken which shades out the sites. It was last recorded on Great Ganilly about 1967 and on St Martin's about 1980, but there is no reason to suppose that it does not still occur on Scilly.

The Scilly Bee

Nine bumblebees have been recorded on Scilly out of the 25 British species. The most interesting is the Island Carder or Scilly Bee, which some people consider to be a separate Scillonian sub-species (ssp. *scyllonius*) of *Bombus muscorum*. However, it may be just a darker variety of the mainland form, which has been found on the islands of western Scotland and Ireland, as well as on Scilly. The Scilly Bee nests in coastal and heathland habitats and can be seen flying round Sea Holly and Common Knapweed, as well as various thistles and heathers. It appears to have declined in abundance and there appear to be no precisely located records for Scilly since 1980.

BUTTERFLIES AND MOTHS

Twenty-three butterflies and over 500 moths have been recorded on Scilly. New species occasionally fly across the sea from Cornwall or Brittany. Some of these may colonise Scilly, others will find no suitable habitat and never be more than occasional visitors. The islands are excellent places from which to observe species from Europe and further south, and the influx of migrant birds is often accompanied by exotic moths such as Old World Webworm, Porter's Rustic, the Delicate, the Gem and Humming-bird Hawk-moth. The maritime climate encourages moths to have more broods per year than they might in colder northern Britain, e.g. Willow Beauty and Light Emerald. The mild weather allows the L-album Wainscot to survive here in two broods a year, whereas in much of Britain it cannot survive the cold winters. Early sightings of Red Admirals are likely to be of hibernating individuals which have successfully over-wintered, although it is possible that the winters are often too mild and wet for them to survive until the spring.

Some of the resident moths have special colour forms. A large proportion of the Lesser Yellow Underwings are strongly marked with prominent dentate cross-lines (this form has been named *sagittifer*). The Feathered Ranunculus and Shuttle-shaped Dart have darker, prettier forms than occur on mainland Britain.

L-album Wainscot

Three nationally rare moths occur on the Isles of Scilly, including the Yellow V moth, *Homoeosoma nimbella* (recorded on St Mary's in 1993) and *Nothris congressariella*, which is restricted by the distribution of its foodplant Balm-leaved Figwort, itself a nationally rare species.

There are 11 resident butterflies on Scilly. Some species on Scilly probably have a single large permanent colony surrounded by satellite populations that become extinct and are then re-colonised.

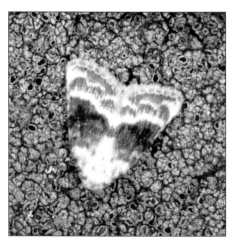

Kent Black Arches

Common Blue

Meadow Brown   *Speckled Wood*   Beth Tonkin

Highly mobile butterflies such as Peacock, Small Tortoiseshell and Small White will move around Scilly with ease and may be regularly seen from the passenger ferries moving between the islands. The Small Copper is one of the commonest butterflies late in the year; the blue-spotted form *caeruleopunctata* occurs in small numbers. More recent arrivals include the Holly Blue, a well-known wanderer, but not recorded on Scilly until 1977 (St Mary's) and 1978 (Tresco). Despite its name, the larval foodplant is likely to be Gorse, Ivy, and possibly *Hebe*. The Comma is another wanderer and may be a recent arrival, following its expansion over the last 80 years in southern Britain.

Other butterflies are more sedentary, such as the Green-veined White and Common Blue, and are therefore more likely to be prone to local extinctions. Ford and Dowdeswell suggested in 1938 that the 300 metre sea gap between Tean and St Martin's prevented movement of Common Blues between the islands. Some of the less mobile British species, e.g. the Hairstreaks and the Skippers, have never been recorded here, although several of them could probably survive once they reached the islands.

The islands are excellent places to see migrant butterflies such as the Painted Lady and the Clouded Yellow. The Large Tortoiseshell recorded floating on the sea off Tresco in 1934 after a south-easterly gale was certainly a migrant. Sightings of Monarchs are rare; occasionally individuals will be carried by southerly winds from the Canary Islands. Red Admirals are also migrants, flying northwards from continental Europe in spring and southwards again from mid-August onwards.

Meadow Brown

The Meadow Brown on Scilly is generally brighter than the mainland race and is a separate subspecies *Maniola jurtina cassiteridum*, similar to the Irish subspecies. It is a common species in Scilly and can be abundant where it occurs. For example, Dowdeswell & Ford estimated that there were 8650 Meadow Browns flying on Tean in 1938. Meadow Browns have been recorded on St Helens, Tresco, St Martins, Tean, Great Arthur, White Island, St Mary's, Gugh, and Great Ganilly

Speckled Wood

The Speckled Wood was first recorded on Scilly at Tresco in 1903 and is now common on the larger islands. It is a separate subspecies *Pararge aegeria insula*, with orange rather than yellow markings, more like the southern European subspecies than the mainland British butterfly. However, these differences can appear slight, especially on old worn specimens where the colour has faded. Although a woodland edge species in much of Britain, in the maritime climate of Scilly Speckled Woods are generally associated with any area where shade occurs, e.g. by hedgerows and isolated trees, and its bright colour may be an adaptation to this more open habitat.

Yellow V Moth   *Oinophila v-flava*

This distinctive moth is about 10mm long and has a distinctive yellowish-white V mark on the brown forewings. It is generally found in warm temperate regions, so that in Britain it is generally confined to warehouses and cellars (where it feeds on fungus and wine corks). However, it occurs in the open on the Isles of Scilly, where it has been recorded on Tresco, St Mary's, St Martin's and St Agnes. The larvae feed on dry vegetable matter (e.g. old grass cuttings) and under the bark on *Pittosporum crassifolium*, which has been widely planted on the islands as a windbreak.

Black-banded Moth

BUTTERFLIES RECORDED ON SCILLY

NAME	RESIDENT/MIGRANT	SUMMARY OF RECORDS
Bath White	M	(St Mary's in 1977)
Brimstone	M	(recorded in 1911)
Camberwell Beauty	M	(St Mary's in 1983)
Clouded Yellow	M	(widely recorded migrant)
Comma	R	(first recorded in 1971, and then in 1981 and 1982)
Common Blue	R	(regularly recorded)
Green-veined White	R?	(sporadically recorded, e.g. on Gugh, St Mary's)
Holly Blue	R	(first recorded in 1977)
Large Tortoiseshell	M	(Tresco in 1934)
Large White	R/M	(widely recorded)
Meadow Brown	R	(widely recorded)
Monarch	M	(occasional, e.g. 1995)
Orange-tip	M?	(recorded on St Mary's in 1986)
Painted Lady	M	(regularly recorded)
Pale Clouded Yellow	M	(rare migrant)
Peacock	R	(widely recorded)
Red Admiral	M	(regularly recorded)
Small Copper	R	(widely recorded)
Small Heath	M	(rare)
Small Tortoiseshell	R	(widely recorded)
Small White	R/M	(widely recorded)
Speckled Wood	R	(widely recorded)
Wall	R	(occasional)

Brussles Lace caterpillar on lichen

Bedstraw Hawk-moth

HOVERFLIES

At least 27 species of hoverfly have been recorded on the Isles of Scilly in recent years, including the Large Narcissus Fly *Merodon equestris*, which is an agricultural pest. In the wild it is harmless, laying its eggs on bluebells, but on Scilly it causes tremendous damage on the bulb fields. The larvae live inside the bulbs for about 300 days before pupating in the soil. There has been a major population surge of Large Narcissus Fly after the withdrawal for environmental reasons of the insecticide Aldrin and these hoverflies have been found on all the main islands where bulbs are grown. Bulb growers try to avoid bulb infestation by planting sterilised bulbs in isolated areas, but these hoverflies are quick to colonise new areas and can be seen flying anytime between April to June.

REPTILES AND AMPHIBIANS

Scilly has possibly 2-3 out of 13 terrestrial species in Britain. The Common Frog is plentiful on some islands. Toads are absent, although toad bones have been found dating from the Later Bronze Age and the 17th century. There are a few recent records of Common Toad from St Mary's and St Agnes, but these may be the result of mistaken identification or records of introduced animals. Like Ireland, there are no snakes. There are occasional records of Slow-worm, probably of individuals which have escaped (slowly!) from captivity. Palmate Newts have been recorded since about 1960. The islands are occasionally visited by turtles, most commonly the Leathery Turtle. This large dark turtle with ridges on its carapace has been recorded here at least 7 times between 1916 and 1985. Two (possibly five) Loggerheads have been seen, including one young specimen washed up alive on St Mary's in 1936 which is now displayed in the Isles of Scilly Museum. A single Kemp's Ridley was reported in 1925 somewhere from Scilly.

Adrian Spalding monitoring insects at Peninnis Head
Pam Tompsett

Cormorants

Scilly is one of the most well known bird-watching localities in Britain and the islands are famous for the large number of rare migrant species that have been recorded here. However, the islands are even more important for their populations of breeding seabirds. A review by the RSPB and English Nature of the most important seabird areas in south western waters identified Scilly as being of international importance for its breeding population of Storm Petrel as well as supporting nationally important numbers of Roseate Tern, Manx Shearwater, Lesser Black-backed Gull and Shag.

BREEDING SEABIRDS

Common Tern
Cormorant
Great Black-backed Gull
Guillemot
Herring Gull
Kittiwake
Lesser Black-backed Gull
Manx Shearwater
Northern Fulmar
Puffin
Razorbill
Roseate Tern
Sandwich Tern
Shag
Storm Petrel

Scilly supports 15 breeding seabirds. Some of these, especially the gulls and the shags, are often present in very large numbers. One of the most impressive sights on Scilly is to see a 'raft' of Shags take flight from the water with perhaps over 300 birds clouding the skyline black until they settle back on the water to fish again. The Western Rocks alone support over 500 pairs and these are far more numerous than their larger relative the Cormorant, of which there are only about 50 pairs in the whole archipelago.

Two of the larger colonies of Lesser Black-backed Gull can be found on Samson (with over 1,000 pairs) and Annet (900 pairs). The Eastern Isles support nearly 500 pairs of Great Black-backed Gull, which breed extensively across the archipelago, as does the Herring Gull. The cliff-nesting Kittiwake is decreasing in numbers on the islands, although the decline is obscured by the tendency of this seabird to move its breeding colonies. This was shown recently by the loss of the traditional Kittiwake breeding site on Chapel Down, St Martin's, and the rapid expansion of a new colony on the Gugh, possibly due to human disturbance or mite infection of nest sites.

Sandwich Tern and Common Tern also breed here, especially on the more sheltered inner archipelago between Samson, Tresco and St Martin's, where they can regularly be seen diving for food.

WADERS

Two species of wader breed on Scilly. Both the Oystercatcher and the Ringed Plover build their nests on or near beaches and hence are susceptible to disturbance during the early summer. The Oystercatcher, locally known as Sea-pies, are colourful raucous birds, soon making their presence known to any visitor straying close to their nest sites. Ringed Plover are quieter and more discreet with their well-camouflaged nests and eggs – so be careful where you walk on peaceful isolated beaches.

PASSERINES

Scilly has fewer than 50 species of breeding birds, other than waders and seabirds. The low diversity is to be expected given the lack of many habitats such as woodland. However, lack of numbers is to some extent compensated for by the tameness and colour variation of many of the birds. For example, in summer Blackbirds on Scilly have distinctive red bills rather than the orange bills of mainland birds. One suggestion for this is that they are dyed red from eating the berries of *Pittosporum* hedges. Even the Wrens, the commonest bird here, have a rustier colour than the mainland form. Fortunately, Scilly is still a stronghold for Song Thrush with numbers four times as high as for comparable areas on the mainland.

Early summer visitors to Scilly will be tantalised by the calling of the Cuckoo, especially in May on St Mary's, St Agnes and St Martin's. Here, over 90% of Cuckoos lay their eggs in the nests of Rock Pipit, a common bird along the coastal edge.

Until recently, the Kestrel was the only bird of prey to breed on the islands, but Peregrine now breeds here. Ravens have only nested on Scilly since 1982 and it is interesting to speculate what the next breeding species to colonise Scilly will be. Choughs were possibly found on St Martin's hundreds of years ago and were shot here at the turn of the century; they currently breed in Wales and in Brittany and may be the next bird to (re-)colonise these islands. In fact, excavations from achaeological sites across Scilly have provided fascinating evidence of the birdlife that previously existed here. Species listed from Bronze Age sites by the Cornwall Archaeological Unit include White Stork, Corncrake, Stone Curlew and Spotted Flycatcher. Larger numbers of wetland species are listed from Iron Age and Romano-British sites.

WINTERING SPECIES

During hard winters on the mainland, Scilly provides a mild refuge for birds unable to feed on frozen ground further east. At these times, large flocks of Redwing, Fieldfare, Lapwing and Golden Plover visit the islands for a short respite and to feed before returning to the mainland. Scilly is also an important staging post for birds on migration between the Arctic Circle and Africa. This was highlighted in the 1984/5 winter when the national winter shorebird count recorded 2,825 waders on Scilly, including 936 Turnstones, 583 Oystercatchers, 326 Sanderlings and 312 Ringed Plovers. Other common wintering species include Purple Sandpipers, Chiffchaff, Blackcap and Black Redstart.

Turnstones   *Beth Tonkin*

MIGRANTS

Scilly has an international reputation for rare birds during the autumn and spring migrations, including many birds from Scandinavia, Siberia and North America. The best time to visit Scilly for these migrants is from late September to early October, "the twitcher season", when birdwatchers hope to catch sight of exotic vagrants such as Yellow-billed Cuckoo, Red-eyed Vireo, Isabelline Shrike, Booted Warbler and Rose-breasted Grosbeak.

Black Poll Warbler　　　　　　*Stuart Hutchings*

Many of these species are blown off-course by gales and arrive on Scilly looking for food and shelter, St Agnes often being the first landfall since North America. There is a similar, but less spectacular event during the spring migration when Scilly is often visited by species that have travelled too far north. Species regularly seen include the colourful and spectacular Hoopoe and Golden Oriele with occasional Bee-eaters to be seen in the islands in May. The appearance of migrant species on Scilly is unpredictable being dependent on wind, weather and chance. The success and continuation of birdwatching here is also dependent on close liaison and co-operation between the birdwatchers and the farming community, a role that is successfully fostered by the Isles of Scilly Environmental Trust.

Upland Sandpiper　　　　　　*Stuart Hutchings*

MANX SHEARWATER

This bird, named after the Isle of Man where it was first recorded in 1014, is an oceanic wanderer only coming on land to breed. It returns to its nest site under cover of darkness, sometimes gathering in colonial rafts on the water just before sunset, especially offshore Annet, one of its major breeding locations. They are magnificent flying birds as they skim the water with minimum wing movement, flicking over to show their black back and then their white bodies. They breed in excavated burrows under the Thrift turf or sometimes use abandoned rabbit burrows. Manx Shearwater colonies on Scilly have been affected by rats predating nests and eggs. To combat this, a small-scale rat-eradication programme has been carried out on some uninhabited islands. In the meantime, this seabird is carefully monitored by controlled trapping and ringing, carried out by licensed experts.

Manx Shearwater

Puffin   Roger Covey

Roseate Tern   David Hunt

PUFFIN

These small comical-looking birds, sometimes called Sea Parrots, are the most popular bird on Scilly. They are the most distinctive species of the Auk family and are readily identified in the breeding season by their bright vividly-coloured beak. These Puffin colonies are the most southerly in Europe. The birds arrive in early spring and nest in cliff-side burrows. The main colony here is on Annet, once supporting over 100,000 birds and called 'Puffin City' on local postcards. In the Middle Ages, salted Puffins were a valuable delicacy, especially as they were considered fish rather than fowl and hence could be eaten on Fridays. In fact, in the 16th century the rent due from Scilly to the Duchy of Cornwall was either 300 Puffins or 6s 8d. Sadly, today Puffin numbers on Scilly including Annet, St Helens and a few other isolated colonies amount to only about 100 pairs. Predation, pollution and lack of food supply are all possible factors behind the decline, emphasising the need for active measures to maintain one of the key birds here. One novel approach to this has been the excavation of man-made burrows on the northern cliffs of St Helens to encourage nesting and breeding here.

ROSEATE TERN

This elegant seabird is one of the rarest in Britain. Breeding numbers on Scilly seldom reach double figures, representing 12% of the British or 1.5% of the European total. It lays its eggs in hollows on rocks or in simple scrapes in sand. The nests are vulnerable to disturbance, water-logging resulting from high tides and storms, and predation by gulls and feral cats, so that in some years no young survive here. Artificial nest sites have been built, vulnerable areas fenced off and rat eradication measures introduced in an attempt to retain and enhance populations of our most threatened breeding seabird.

STORM PETREL

Locally known as Mother Carey's Chicken, the Storm Petrel is a black sparrow-sized bird that flies low over the water and only returns to land at its remote breeding locations under cover of dark. It breeds on boulder beaches on Annet and other isolated islands, where it's characteristic purring and chirping sounds can be heard late at night emanating from colonies deep within the boulders. It is

Storm Petrel
right: Storm Petrel beach

BUDGERIGAR

Several attempts have been made to introduce the budgerigar into the wild in Britain, but feral budgerigars are unlikely to survive the winter without food and shelter. However, winters on Scilly are generally warm enough for the birds to survive and in 1969, following a visit by the Queen Mother to Tresco, 4 pairs of free-flying birds were introduced into an aviary with an exit hole. 6 pairs

almost impossible to accurately census this bird but Scilly is thought to support 2-3,000 pairs. The continuing survival of the Storm Petrel on Scilly requires a regime of total isolation and lack of disturbance in the breeding season. The species also requires habitats that are free from rats which predate nest sites. The long term monitoring and ringing programme has shown that the birds regularly fly between Scilly and the islands of Ouessant (Ushant) off the west coast of Brittany, 200 kilometres away.

were added in 1970 and by 1973 the budgerigars (now about 60 pairs) were living and nesting outside the aviary. As the flock increased, aided by artificial feeding, they were occasionally seen on Bryher, St Martin's, St Mary's and St Agnes in the following years. They survived until about 1984; budgerigars no longer fly freely around the islands.

Shags

Guillemots

'Twitchers'   Pat Cashman

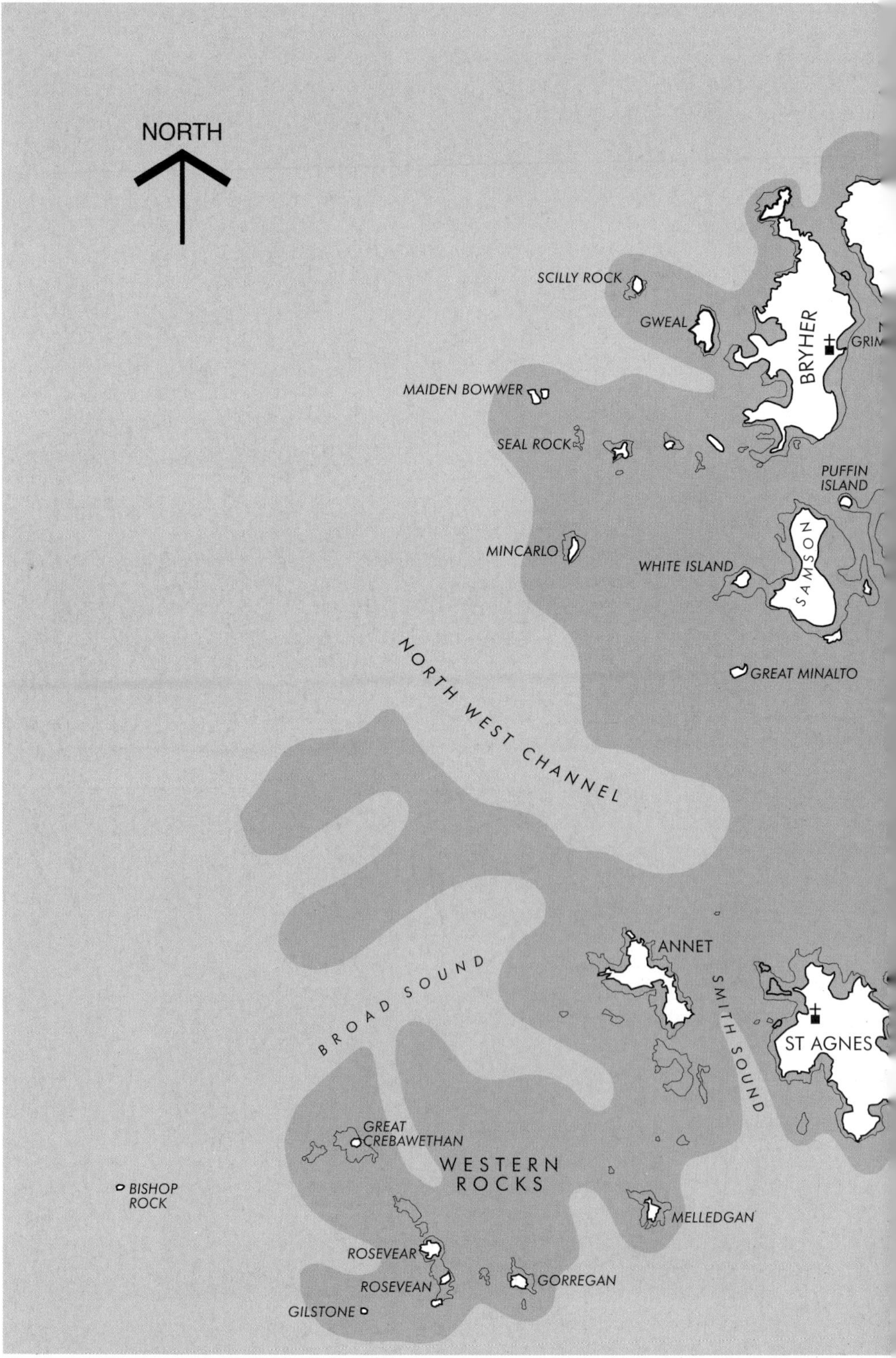

NORTH

SCILLY ROCK

GWEAL

BRYHER

GRIM

MAIDEN BOWWER

SEAL ROCK

PUFFIN
ISLAND

S A M S O N

MINCARLO

WHITE ISLAND

GREAT MINALTO

N O R T H   W E S T   C H A N N E L

ANNET

SMITH SOUND

ST AGNES

B R O A D   S O U N D

GREAT
CREBAWETHAN

W E S T E R N
R O C K S

BISHOP
ROCK

MELLEDGAN

ROSEVEAR

ROSEVEAN

GORREGAN

GILSTONE

ROUND ISLAND

WHITE ISLAND

ST. HELENS

TEAN

ST MARTIN'S

OLD
GRIMSBY

RESCO

EASTERN ISLES

GREAT GANILLY

GREAT POOL

ESCO
BBEY

THE ROAD

CROW SOUND

ST. MARY'S

TOLL'S ISLAND

HUGH TOWN

OLD
TOWN

St Mary's
Airport

Gitstone

ISLES OF SCILLY

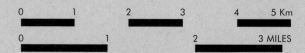

0   1   2   3   4   5 Km

0   1   2   3 MILES

Seven or eight terrestrial mammals have been recorded on Scilly. Moles, foxes, badgers, otters, stoats, weasels, hares and squirrels are absent. Many of the species present here arrived accidentally through human agency, e.g. the Brown and Black Rat. The Black Rat was recorded by Leland in 1538 on Rat Island on St Mary's but is now extinct on the islands. The Brown Rat occurs widely on many of the islands; many of the breeding seabird colonies on Samson have suffered from predation of eggs by rats. However, a recent major rat eradication programme has been initiated to make the island rat-free. The Field or Wood Mouse has been recorded on St Mary's and Tresco, perhaps accidentally imported by early settlers or perhaps to Tresco as late as the time when Tresco Abbey house and gardens were built. The Hedgehog was deliberately introduced to St Mary's. Rabbits are widespread, and form an essential part of the island ecology. They have been on Scilly from before 1176, and were probably introduced for meat and skins. Pipistrelle Bats have been found at low densities on all five inhabited islands, with records from Tresco dating back to 1904; Whiskered or Brandt's Bats may be present on Tresco. There is no doubt that bat populations have declined in recent years, perhaps due to the use of insecticides on bulb fields and the renovation of derelict buildings.

POLAR BEARS ON SCILLY

Perhaps the most unusual record is of a possible dead Polar Bear in 1966! According to a report in *The Cornishman* on 18th August 1966, several small boats went out to look at something large, shaggy and white seen floating between the islands. Despite prodding it with boat hooks, no one was prepared to claim that it was definitely a Polar Bear and it was last seen floating southwards through St Mary's Sound. However, in response to this report there was a claim that something large, white and covered with sand, looking like a Polar Bear, was seen coming out of the sea near the sand bar on Gugh on 3rd June 1966. When searched for later, it had disappeared.

LESSER WHITE TOOTHED SHREW

The Scilly Shrew is about 7-8cm long and weighs about 7 grams. It is similar to the Common Shrew (which is not found on Scilly) but has white teeth, more prominent ears and a bristly tail. It exists on Scilly as a separate sub-species *Crocidura suaveolens cassiteridum* or the Lesser White-toothed Shrew and was named after the Cassiterides, the island – wrongly assumed to be Scilly - from which the Phoenicians allegedly obtained their tin.

It is now generally considered that the Scilly Shrew reached these islands by chance introduction, probably from the Mediterranean, and may have been on the islands since the Bronze Age. They have been recorded recently from St Mary's, St Martin's, Bryher, Samson, Tresco, St Agnes and Annet, and there are earlier records for Tean and Gugh. It has been suggested that their habitat of feeding on Sand-hoppers and insects amongst the strandline kelp on beaches suggests that they may have been transported in recent times around the islands hidden amongst seaweed used as manure.

Scilly Shrew is Britain's rarest shrew, with a population estimated at about 99,000. Threats to their survival include habitat loss due to development, predation by rats and domestic cats, but it is possible that numbers of Scilly Shrew have been increasing since the 1970s.

The Scilly Shrew

MARINE LIFE

The marine waters of Scilly are remote from the mainland, little disturbed by man and with little or no fluvial sediment or freshwater input. This pollution-free environment, with clear water, mild oceanic climate and a wide variety of habitats (from exposed rocks to sheltered sand flats) has resulted in a rich and diverse marine wildlife. Scilly is the only Lusitanean archipelago in England and its south west location means that there are an abundance of Mediterranean-Atlantic species that are uncommon or absent elsewhere in the country. Conversely, however, the isolation of the islands, the granite bedrock, deep water and strong tidal currents have all combined to limit the range of marine life when compared with more easterly coasts and islands such as Lundy. Scilly therefore has an assemblage of marine life unique in Britain.

The outstanding importance of the marine life of Scilly was confirmed in 1989 when the whole of the seabed contained within the 50m depth contour was declared a Voluntary Marine Park, established to "conserve and protect the ecological, archaeological, historical and environmental heritage". It is managed by a committee comprising the Isles of Scilly Environmental Trust, the Duchy of Cornwall, the Sea Fisheries Committee, the Council of the Isles of Scilly and English Nature.

More recently, the international importance of certain marine habitats, especially the inter-tidal sand flats and sedimentary shores, has been highlighted by their proposed designation as a Marine Special Area of Conservation (SAC) under the EC Habitats and Species Directive. The Marine Park and Marine SAC aim to ensure "harmonious co-existence with traditional local communities to the mutual benefit of the marine environment, local community and visitors to the islands". To assist this a leaflet describing the aims of the Marine Park and an associated Code of Conduct has been made freely available on the islands.

The archipelago exhibits both rocky and sedimentary shores and sub-littoral habitats with their associated communities and species. The four areas of particular importance within the Marine Park are:

* St Martins, Tresco and Samson Flats
* St Agnes and Annet

* The east coast of St Mary's
* The Western Rocks

ROCKY SHORES AND SUB-LITTORAL HABITATS

Scilly has some of the most exposed and spectacular rocky shores in Britain, open to the full force of the western Atlantic. Out on the Western Rocks, the marine life has adapted to survive extreme gale force conditions. Several rare species are found on these exposed shores including the red algae *Schmitzia hiscockiana* (found in Scilly in 1983) and the only British location for the Orange-peel bryozoan *Turbicellepora magnicostata*. At some

The Marine Park, protected area around the Islands

Goose barnacles

sites the lichen-dominated splash zone extends up to 11m above tidal datum. Overall, some 128 algae, 13 lichens and 237 animal species have been recorded from these rocky shores.

On the more sheltered rocky shores, brown algae dominate and a typical zonation occurs with Spiral Wrack *Fucus spiralis* at the top of the shore merging into Bladder Wrack *Fucus vesiculosus* and the Serrated Wrack *Fucus serratus* on the lower shore. Further down the brown algae merge into

beds of kelp, with red algae, sponges and ascidians only uncovered at low water spring tides. On Scilly, the rocky shores have abundant top shells including the Painted Topshell *Calliostoma zizyphinum*, the Flat Topshell *Gibbula umbilicalis* and the brightly coloured Flat Periwinkle *Littorina obtusata*. Surprisingly, the Common Periwinkle *Littorina littorea* is absent from Scilly and the Common Barnacle *Semibalanus balanoides* is rare, although species of the barnacle *Chthamalus* do occur. The Common Mussel *Mytilus edulis* is also rare on Scilly and very small in size where it does occur. These absences are probably due to the predominantly west to east currents.

Below the tidal limits on the rocky slopes are found the dense kelp forests dominated by Thongweed *Himanthalia elongata*, Dabberlocks *Alaria esculenta*, Oarweed *Laminaria digitata* and *Saccorhiza polyschides*. These deeper water species are often washed up on the beach, especially after gales have ripped their holdfasts from the rocky substrate. There are several rarities, including *Pikea californica,* which is a Pacific species first recorded in the north east Atlantic on Scilly and which is thought to have arrived here on the floats of flying boats during the Second World War. The islands also contain numerous sub-tidal rocky reefs, swept by strong tidal currents. These often support a rich fauna including sponges, sea squirts and hydroids. Here are found the sponges *Axinella damicornis, Tethyspira spinosa* and *Desmacidon*

Kelp Forest

fruticosum. Deep sheltered bedrock off the east coast of St Mary's supports *Parerythropodium coralloides* and the slow-growing spectacular Sea Fan *Eunicella verrucosa*. The clear waters also allow the southern species of kelp *Laminaria ochroleuca* to grow rapidly at depths of up to 30m. Deep water caves, overhangs and crevices support other southern species including the algae *Asparagopsis armata* and the exotically-named Red Sea Fingers *Alcyonium glomeratum*.

SEDIMENT SHORES AND SUB-LITTORAL HABITATS

The marine sediments within the archipelago are derived from the erosion and decomposition of granite. Therefore, many of the deposits consist of coarse sand and gravels, merging into more stable fine sand sediments. Interestingly, the coarse sediments on Scilly which are sheltered from wave action support rich communities of burrowing animals, including species more typical of subtidal sediments elsewhere. There are also areas of submerged peats and humic silts that represent the prehistoric land surfaces that were inundated as a result of rising sea levels.

There are four main areas of sediment shore on Scilly. They are all easily accessible at low water and are located:

- east of Samson

- between Bryher and Tresco

- off Old Grimsby on the east side of Tresco

- on the south side of St Martin's

They support a rich and diverse range of intertidal communities and are especially important for their burrowing worms, molluscs and sea urchins.

The marine life of intertidal areas varies with the sediment type, wave exposure and tidal currents. The St Martin's flats are the largest and most diverse area of sand exposed at low water within Scilly. All of the lower sediment shores have dense beds of burrowing heart urchins including the Sea Potato *Echinocardium cordatum*, *Echinocyamus pusillus* and the Purple Heart Urchin *Spatangus purpureus*. These are all species that are normally not found above mean low water except on Scilly. The burrowing bivalve molluscs include the Thin Tellin, Rayed Artemis and the Razor Shell. Lugworm, Sand Mason Worm and other polychaete worms are abundant here as evidenced by the numerous small holes and excavated debris across the lower and mid-shore areas. Large populations of burrowing sea anemones occur in the more sheltered locations and can be seen emergent and colourful as the tide returns across the unique intertidal habitats. Most of the sediments are too mobile to support plants and algae although the more sheltered upper shores and mudflats are dominated by the bright green algae *Enteromorpha* which is especially prominent during the summer.

Beds of Eelgrass *Zostera marina* occur on stable sandflats, with a rich variety of associated plants and animals encouraged by the sheltered conditions and sediment stability, e.g. molluscs, polychaetes and the sea anemone *Anthopleura ballii*. Unusual species of algae are also found here including *Jania rubens* and the southern species

Sea urchins for sale

Asparagopsis armata. Other burrowing animals include molluscs, amphipods and burrowing anemones. Elsewhere the bivalve *Callista chione* occurs in sublittoral fine sand habitats, as does the seasquirt *Molgula oculata.* The rare chiton *Leptochiton scabridus* has been recorded on stones in coarse sand deposits.

EELGRASS *ZOSTERA MARINA*

Eelgrass is one of the very few species of flowering plants that can tolerate living in the sea in both intertidal and subtidal habitats but requires sheltered fine-grained sediment. In Scilly, it occurs in several locations including St Mary's harbour and the Tresco channel, but the largest beds occur offshore Old Grimsby on Tresco. Eelgrass is totally different from true seaweeds or marine algae with flat, long, narrow leaves between 0.5 and 1cm wide and to 1m in length. It is dark or grass green and produces inconspicuous flowers and seed rather like terrestrial grasses.

It provides a sheltered habitat for other species of plants and animals and is one of the most species-rich of the marine habitats. The leaves of Eelgrass provide a unique habitat for the rare hydroid *Laomedea angulata*, the sea snail *Jujubinus striatus*

and the Stalked Jellyfish *Haliclystus auricula.* Its roots are particularly susceptible to erosion during storm conditions and uprooted leaves are commonly found along the wrack line. In recent years, it has suffered disease and die-back, but the cause of these problems has not yet been identified.

CETACEANS

Numerous species of cetacean have been recorded for Scilly, many of them washed up as dead corpses. Schools of the Common Dolphin are often seen offshore, especially from the decks of the *Scillonian.* The Harbour Porpoise is a more infrequent visitor and Risso's Dolphin is occasionally recorded at sea. Other cetaceans washed up around the islands include Long-finned Pilot Whale, Killer Whale, Bottle-nosed Dolphin and more rarely the Sperm Whale. Bones collected from these dead animals can be seen ornamenting gardens throughout the islands especially in the cottages at New Grimsby on Tresco.

GREY SEAL

Scilly provides the most southerly breeding ground for Grey Seals with a population of about 250. This is the largest wild mammal in Britain, the male bulls often reaching over 2m in length and weighing over 200kg. The largest concentrations on Scilly occur on the Western Rocks, Norrard Rocks and in the Eastern Isles. Seals come ashore on these rocky exposed islands to pup between September and December, producing about 80 pups a year. Many of the seals are resident, but others migrate around the British coast and the Channel Islands, as far as France. Scilly is an excellent place for seal-watching, as they laze on their favourite haul-out rocks and ledges at low tide or go bobbing and bottling (floating vertically) in the water. Recent monitoring by tagging and diagnostic face/body marking identification indicates that despite natural high seal-pup mortality the population of these beautiful creatures here is relatively stable.

Grey Seal

EXOTIC VAGRANTS, FLOTSAM AND JETSAM

The location of Scilly has resulted in a wide variety of exotic plants and animal species being washed up around its shores. The lists include:

Mediterranean-Atlantic species

Mediterranean Purple Sea-urchin	*Sphaerechinus granularis*
Seahorse	*Hippocampus ramulosus*
Puffer-fish	*Lagocephalus lagocephalus*
Trigger-fish	*Balistes carolinensis*
Marbled Electric Ray	*Torpedo marmorata*
Sun-fish	*Mola mola*
Pink Tunny	*Luva luva*
Swordfish	*Xiphias gladius*

Caribbean and the Gulf of Mexico species

Sail Fish	*Istiophorus platypterus*
Blue Marlin	*Makaira nigricans*
Leatherback Turtle	*Dermochelys coriacea*
Loggerhead Turtle	*Caretta caretta*
Sea Heart (Lucky Bean)	*Entada gigas*
Horse-eye Bean	*Macuna urens*

Southern Species

Wreckfish	*Polyprion americanus*
Grey Shark	*Hexanchus griseus*
Porbeagle	*Lamna nasmo*
Basking Shark	*Cetorhinus maximus*
By-the-wind Sailor	*Velella velella*
Violet Sea-snail	*Janthina janthina*

Sea-balls of Neptune Grass *Posidonia oceanica*

Neptune Grass, a sea-grass similar to Eelgrass, does not occur in Scilly but is found in the Mediterranean and north to the Bay of Biscay. However, broken leaves of the plant when mixed with sand and rolled about in the waves can form soft small brown balls, some about 4-6mm in diameter. These are commonly known as 'sea-balls' and can occasionally be found along the high tide mark around the islands.

ANNET

Annet is the largest uninhabited island on the western side of the archipelago. Located 1 km west of St Agnes, it is only one kilometre long from the granite stacks at the Haycocks to Annet Neck in the south. The island is composed of Hercynian granite overlain by raised beach deposits and prominent boulder storm beaches, particularly along the western coast. The island is low lying, reaching a maximum altitude of 18m. Exposure to wind and salt spray has restricted species diversity and only 53 species of vascular plant have been recorded here. Thrift occurs in abundance, forming a continuous hummocky turf over most of the northern end of the island where it represents one of the best developed examples of Thrift turf in the British Isles. Recent invasion of the Thrift turf by extensive stands of Yorkshire Fog and Bracken urgently needs to be controlled.

In the southern half of the island the areas of deeper soil support Bracken, together with Lesser Celandine and Bluebell. The boulder-strewn beaches support Sea Beet and Tree Mallow. The nationally rare Shore Dock occurs on shingle beaches in the south. The exposed granite carns and boulder beaches support a variety of rare maritime lichen species including the nationally rare *Roccella fuciformis*.

Annet is of outstanding importance as a seabird colony and supports eleven species of breeding seabirds. Two of these species, Storm Petrel and Lesser Black-backed Gull, reach nationally important breeding populations. The Storm Petrels breed in the older and more stable granite boulder beaches particularly along the western and southern sides of the island, whilst the Lesser Black-backed Gull colony is mainly concentrated in the Bracken-Bluebell vegetation south-west of Carn Windlass. The other breeding seabirds include the largest colonies in the archipelago of Manx Shearwater, Puffin, and Great Black-backed Gull together with Razorbill, Fulmar, Common Tern, Herring Gull, Kittiwake and Shag.

Because of its importance for breeding seabirds, access to Annet is not permitted during the breeding season except by special permit. However, the daily tripper boats provide excellent vantage points for viewing the Puffins and other wildlife. In addition on summer-evenings 'rafts' of Manx Shearwaters can be seen gathering on the water offshore from Annet prior to flying onto the island under cover of dusk.

Annet

BRYHER

Shipman Head

"Waved" maritime heath covers much of the central part of Shipman Head Down, with Heather, Bell Heather and Western Gorse. European Gorse forms extensive scrub along the south side of the Downs. Above some of the coves and along the coastal edge, areas of more species-rich maritime grassland occur, with Thrift, Buck's-horn Plantain, Yorkshire Fog and Spring Squill. The nationally rare Orange Bird's-foot and Hairy Bird's-foot-trefoil can be found here, together with a range of lichens such as Lungwort and Golden Hair-lichen. The isolated promontory is an important seabird colony site with large colonies of Kittiwake and Herring Gull. Razorbill and Shag also breed here and Ringed Plover breed on the open heathland.

Rushy Bay and Heathy Hill

These areas on the southern end of Bryher consist of a low exposed granite hill (rising to about 10m above sea level) backed by a small sand dune and dune grassland overlying a storm boulder beach. The dune grassland is particularly important for the rare Dwarf Pansy. The species-rich dune grassland has abundant Sand Sedge, Buck's-horn Plantain, Sea Stork's-bill, Red Fescue and Thrift, as well as the nationally scarce Sea Spurge, Portland Spurge and Western Clover. Sea Beet is abundant on the dune edges where the low dunes are dominated by Marram with Sea Holly. Sea Kale grows on the boulder and cobble strandline at the back of Stony Porth. The exposed summit of Heathy Hill supports a small area of low, wind-

Waved maritime heath

pruned heathland dominated by Heather, Bell Heather and Western Gorse. Rare plants found here include Orange Bird's-foot, Small Adder's-tongue and Autumn Lady's-tresses. The deeper soils on the hillside support Bracken, Honeysuckle and Bramble. Maritime grassland with abundant Thrift, Sea Beet and Buck's-horn Plantain occurs around the coastal margins of the hill and out towards Droppy Nose Point. The top of Samson Hill to the east of Rushy Bay provides a panoramic view of most of the archipelago and is well worth the short, steep climb.

Pool of Bryher and Popplestone Bank

The Pool (Great Pool) is the only true brackish lagoon within Scilly, being separated from the sea by a narrow highly mobile storm beach backed by a small dune system. Grey Mullet can often be seen swimming in the Pool and the lagoon. The shallow water supports a dense growth of Beaked Tasselweed and Sea Milkwort. Saltmarsh Rush is abundant around the margins of the pool with Lesser Sea-spurrey and Red Goosefoot in the ad-

Shipman Head, Bryher

jacent turf. Little Pool, a small pond to the north, is less brackish and supports abundant Lesser Marshwort and Brackish Water-crowfoot in the open water, with Intermediate Water Starwort, Lesser Spearwort and Marsh Pennywort around the margins.

The storm beach backing Great Popplestone is one of the more dynamic on Scilly and has been breached by winter gales on several occasions. Newly erected coast protection measures, using granite blocks imported from Cornwall, are aimed at slowing down the rate of coastal retreat and protecting the adjacent homes, hotel and fresh water supply. The narrow coastal dune system behind is dominated by Marram; inland of this is an area of dune grassland with Sand Sedge, Red Fescue, Buck's-horn Plantain, Thrift, Common Stork's-bill and Wild Carrot. The nationally rare Early Meadow-grass occurs here.

THE EASTERN ISLES

The Eastern Isles are located on the north eastern edge of the archipelago immediately to the southeast of St Martins. These islands include the uninhabited islands of Great Ganilly, Little Ganilly, Great Arthur, Little Arthur, Nornour, Great Ganinick, Great Innisvouls and Menawethan, together with a number of smaller adjacent islets and rocks.

All are composed of coarse grained Hercynian granite with small areas of wind-blown sand and shingle bars. Although the islands are partially sheltered from extreme westerly gales, their low altitude, maritime exposure and thin podzolic soils have resulted in a depleted flora. Great Ganilly, the largest and highest island covering about 13 hectares and reaching a height of about 34 metres, has 74 recorded plant species out of a list of 111 for the whole of the Eastern Isles. The nationally rare Orange Bird's-foot occurs in the small area of maritime heathland dominated by Bell Heather on the northern side of the island. The steep slopes of the islands are covered by Bracken and Bramble whilst many of the lower outer margins are fringed with maritime grassland where Thrift and Sea Beet are abundant. Small areas of blown sand linking Great, Middle and Little Arthur support stands of Marram Grass. Sea Kale occurs in the backshore zone between Nornour and Great Ganilly. Other uncommon plants on the islands include White Ramping Fumitory and Sea Radish, together with the nationally rare Balm-leaved Figwort and Shore Dock.

Great Ganinick is the only island on Scilly, apart from Tresco, where Oak trees have been recorded in recent times. Butcher's Broom also occurs here and on Nornour, and is perhaps associated with the previous Roman occupation and settlement.

Several species of breeding seabirds live on the islands, including large colonies of Great Black-backed Gull, Lesser Black-backed Gull, Herring Gull and Shag. There are smaller colonies of Razorbill, Cormorant, Fulmar and a few Puffin. The Eastern Isles also provide isolated habitats for an important breeding colony of Grey Seal.

Eastern Isles

The bar at Gugh

GUGH

Gugh is a small, partly inhabited island connected to the east side of St Agnes by a sandy bar, flooded at high tide. The island is only one kilometre long, rising to 34 metres on Kittern Hill and underlain by Hercynian granite covered by shallow podzolic soils on the higher land with deeper soils on the lower slopes. A small area of blown sand has accumulated at the eastern end of the Bar.

Wind pruned, 'waved' maritime heath (dominated by Heather, Bell Heather and Western Gorse) covers much of the high ground on Gugh. The southern area also includes a population of the nationally rare Orange Bird's-foot growing in heathland rich in rare lichen species, including Lungwort and the Golden Hair-lichen.

Maritime grassland with abundant Thrift occurs in the north of the island and along the coastal edge. The nationally rare Early Meadow-grass, the uncommon Western Clover and Adder's-tongue occur in the short turf areas around the coastal margin of Gugh. The blown sand at the end of the Bar supports a small dune system with Marram and Sand Couch dominant. The adjacent dune grassland has Sand Sedge, Portland Spurge and the only record in Scilly for Viper's-bugloss. The central area of Gugh is dominated by Bracken with a large population of the nationally rare Balm-leaved Figwort.

Common Tern used to breed on the heathland on the south of the island and there is also a large colony of Lesser Black-backed Gull here. In recent years, Kittiwake have built up a large colony on the north-east side of Gugh and visitors are asked to avoid this area in the breeding season. Other breeding seabirds include Herring Gull and Great Black-backed Gull. On the shores there are also breeding Ringed Plover and records of Storm Petrel and Manx Shearwater.

Three notable invertebrates occur on Gugh: the woodlouse *Trichoniscoides saeroeensis*, the centipede *Geophilus osquidatum* and the moth Kent Black Arches, which has been recently rediscovered here.

NORRARD ROCKS

Norrard (Northern) Rocks lie on the north western edge of the archipelago immediately to the west of Bryher and Samson. They are comprised of a series of small uninhabited granite islands including Gweal, Scilly Rock, Maiden Bower, Castle Bryher, Illiswilgig and Mincarlo together with numerous other isolated rocks and ledges. All of the islands are low lying, reaching a maximum height of only 32 metres on Gweal and hence they are all exposed to the full force of south west gales from the Atlantic and excessive salt spray.

The shallow skeletal soils are mainly confined to the larger islands; elsewhere soil is only found in sheltered, isolated pockets in the granite. Because of the thin soils and the extreme exposure, only six species of vascular plant have been recorded from the outer islands: Tree Mallow, Thrift, Sea Beet, Common Scurvygrass, Rock Sea-spurrey and Orache. On some islets, such as Maiden Bower, there are no flowering plants. Norrard Rocks are of particular importance for their seabird colonies, supporting 10 species of breeding seabirds. Mincarlo is of particular note as it supports the largest colony of Cormorant on Scilly. Puffin breed on Mincarlo, Castle Bryher and Scilly Rock and there is a large breeding colony of Shag throughout Norrard Rocks. Other breeding seabirds include Fulmar, Razorbill, Guillemot, Great Black-backed Gull, Lesser Black-backed Gull and Herring Gull. There are also records of Storm Petrel breeding on Mincarlo. The isolated rocks and islands of Norrard Rocks are one of the most important breeding sites on Scilly for Grey Seal.

Landing on Norrard Rocks can be difficult and access is not permitted during the bird breeding season, although the tripper boats provide excellent views and informed commentary.

ROUND ISLAND

This island, dominated by its conspicuous lighthouse seen from many different vista around the island, supports important colonies of Storm Petrel and Peregrine.

ST AGNES

St Agnes, or Agnes as it is more commonly referred to, is the most western of the inhabited islands. It exhibits a wide variety of wildlife habitats. The central farmed area has extensive planted shelter belts (really "fences" of hedging plants) that are particularly important for providing cover for many of the rare migrant bird species that reach Scilly during spring and autumn. For birds on migration, or blown off-course from the east coast of North America, Agnes provides the first land fall site of western Europe, and the bird list for this island is the largest and most exotic on Scilly. This is also true of migrant moths.

Big Pool and Browarth Point

Big Pool and the adjacent Little Pool are the only areas of open water on St Agnes and are separated from the sea by narrow, mobile shingle and boulder beaches, occasionally overtopped during winter gales. The adjacent wet grassland contains a number of rare and notable plant species. Big Pool and Little Pool are mesotrophic (i.e. with average nutrient levels) freshwater habitats with abundant Fennel Pondweed. However the occasional influx of sea water during winter storms and the exposure to salt spray has resulted in some brackish influences reflected in the presence of Saltmarsh Rush and Sea Clubrush around the margins of both pools. Recent analysis of the lake sediments in Big Pool has shown a thick layer of sand thought to have been deposited as a result of the tsunami wave

Coast protection on St Agnes

generated by the Lisbon earthquake of 1st November 1755, some 1000 miles to the south west of Scilly. Two peat bands are also present, the lower being of medieval origin.

The grassland adjacent to the pool contains a rich and diverse flora including Western Clover, Suffocated Clover and Small Adder's Tongue. Adder's Tongue also occurs here in the short turf with Chamomile, Autumn Lady's-tresses, Bristle Clubrush and Subterranean Clover. The nationally rare Early Meadow-grass grows in the drier grassland on the trackway in the southern part of the area. The strandline vegetation at the back of Porth Killier, Porth Coose and Periglis Bay is particularly notable for the populations of Sea Radish and Sea Kale growing in association with Frosted Orache and Babington's Orache.

Ringed Plover breed along these beaches and Mallard, Coot, Gadwall and Moorhen have bred at Big Pool. This is also an important wetland feeding site for birds on passage and it supports small flocks of over-wintering wildfowl, such as Mallard and waders including Turnstone, Sanderling, Redshank, Curlew, Purple Sandpiper and Grey Plover. Grey Plover roosts have been counted by John Hale at St Agnes over the years; in the winter of 1994/95 maximum monthly counts rose from 6 in October to 45 (December), 43 (January) and 53 (February), before falling sharply to 2 in April.

Wingletang Down

On Wingletang Down, thin skeletal and podzolic soils overlie the Hercynian granite which outcrops at the surface to form numerous weathered boulders, tors, and carns on a low plateau no more than 20 metres high. In places, wind-blown sand covers the granite in the low lying area between Beady Pool and Porth Askin. The thin soils and extreme exposure have led to the development of wind pruned 'waved' maritime heath over much of Wingletang Down, dominated by Heather, Bell Heather and Western Gorse. In places the open heathland is being invaded by scrub of European Gorse and Bracken. The heathland is particularly important for the occurrence of a number of nationally rare plants including Least Adder's-tongue, a species restricted in Britain to this site and the Channel Isles, and Orange Bird's-foot. Other notable plants include another Adder's-tongue and Western Clover. There are also strong populations

Autumn Lady's-tresses

of Autumn Lady's Tresses and Bristle Clubrush, a species rare in Scilly. In addition, the nationally rare Early Meadow-grass grows on the short maritime grassland on the coastal edge to the north-west of the downs.

The dune grassland to the south has abundant Sand Sedge, Sand Couch, Portland Spurge and Common Storksbill. Sea Kale occurs in the strandline vegetation at the back of Beady Pool, and Sea-milkwort can be found at Horse Point.

Oystercatchers and Ringed Plover breed at Beady Pool and there is a small breeding colony of Herring Gull along the north-west shore of the downs. There are also records of Storm Petrel and Manx Shearwater breeding in some of the west coast storm boulder beaches.

ST MARTIN'S

The Sedimentary Shore

St Martin's flats form the largest area of sand exposed at mean low water in Scilly. The most important section stretches for 2km along the south west shoreline from the hotel quay to Cruther's Point and extends offshore to Pigs Ledge, Moths Ledge and Round Rock Ledge. The shore is influenced by complex local tidal and current patterns, leading to sediment sorting, periodic reshaping of the shore and a mixture of habitat types and associated communities. St Martin's flats are a moderately exposed sandy shore with bivalve molluscs, burrowing heart urchins and marine worms (polychaetes). The intertidal zone comprises a coarse to medium sand beach with boulders grading through to cobbles and some areas of rocky reef.

This shore is of particular interest as the wildlife found within the lower shores include species, such as the Sea Potato *Echinocardium cordatum*, that are not usually found to extend above mean low water. Other heart urchins occur below mean low water such as the tiny Pea-urchin *Echinocyamus*

pusillus. The surface dwelling animals include the Sandhopper *Talitrus saltator*, together with gastropod snails such as the Common Necklace Shell *Polinices polianus* and the Netted Dog Whelk *Hinia reticulata*. There is a rich range of bivalve molluscs, with species including the Thin Tellin *Angulus tenuis*, the Rayed Artemis *Dosinia exoleta* and the Razor Shell *Ensis arcuatus*. Other species within the sediment include the Lugworm *Arenicola marina* on the mid and lower shore, the Sand Mason Worm *Lanice conchilega* and several other polychaete worms, such as *Scololepis fuliginosa*, *Glycera* sp., *Nephtys* spp. and *Travesia forbesii*. We can also find here the Sea Cucumber *Leptosynapta inhaerens* and the worm-like hemichordate *Glossobalanus sarniensis*. There are several areas of rocky habitat, with boulders and intertidal reefs, which support a variety of important species and communities. This is a fragile site so it is important to replace boulders after looking under them and to take proper precautions when visiting inter-tidal locations.

Chapel Down

Chapel Down forms an exposed headland on the eastern side of the island. The underlying granite forms steep cliffs to the north and east with a 30-35 metre high plateau inland, covered in thin soils clothed with distinctive "waved" maritime heathland, dominated by low prostrate ridges of Heather, Bell Heather and Western Gorse, with Tormentil, Heath Bedstraw, Common Bird's-foot-trefoil, Pignut and English Stonecrop. The nationally rare Orange Bird's-foot and Hairy Bird's-foot-trefoil occur here. The soils are deeper in the more sheltered places of the plateau, where Bracken, Bramble and Honeysuckle scrub clothe the slopes. Small areas of maritime grassland occur along the coastal edge with Thrift, Sea Beet, Sorrel and Buck's-horn Plantain. Rare lichens occur on the granite cliffs, including *Roccella fuciformis* and Golden Hair-lichen. There is a large breeding colony of Kittiwake, together with Fulmar, Herring Gull and Lesser Black-backed Gull. Unfortunately, the maritime heathland is being threatened by invasive Bracken and European Gorse, which increases the risk of accidental fires, so new wide firebreaks are maintained on this site in conjunction with scrub control in order to reduce the risk of fire.

Raised beach at Porth Seal

Great Bay & White island

The Plains and Great Bay

Great Bay is an east-facing beach on the north side of the island, where a dune system has developed on wind-blown granite sand. The site is also important for illustrating the classic succession of coastal communities from embryo dunes to dune scrub. The embryo dunes support a well developed strandline vegetation, where Sea Sandwort, Frosted Orache and Sea Rocket are common. The dunes behind are dominated by Sand Couch and Marram, with Sea Holly, Sea Spurge and Portland Spurge. Further inland, the species-rich dune grassland is important for the occurrence of Orange Bird's-foot in a low rabbit-grazed sward, where Thrift, Red Fescue, Sea Stork's-bill and Eyebright are common. The heathland is dominated by Heather, Bell Heather and Western Gorse, often with a conspicuous lichen ground flora with *Cladonia* species. Towards the top of The Plains, Western Gorse and European Gorse form extensive scrub, with Bracken, Bramble, Wood Sage and Honeysuckle on the deeper soils towards Frenchmen's Graves. Ringed Plover breed here. Unfortunately, the cessation of grazing here and variations in the rabbit population have led to a rapid expansion of European Gorse to the detriment of the rarer plants.

Hedges on St Martin's

ST HELEN'S, NORTHWETHEL, FOREMANS ISLAND AND MEN-A-VAUR

The St Helen's group of small uninhabited islands lie on the northern edge of the archipelago. St Helen's, the largest, rises to over 40 metres. Northwethel and Foremans Island are partially sheltered between Tresco and St Martins, but the steep rocky islet of Men-a-vaur to the north is fully exposed to the Atlantic gales. All of the islands are composed of well-jointed Hercynian granite, eroded to form the prominent gullies that traverse Men-a-vaur but covered with deep soils on the lower slopes of St Helen's and Northwethel. These deeper soils are dominated by Bracken and Bramble but with a significant population of the nationally rare Balm-leaved Figwort.

The summit of St Helen's has thin soils with maritime heathland adjacent to lichen-rich granite outcrops. The heathland shows the effects of previous fire damage where Heather and Bell Heather are colonising more open areas dominated by Buck's-horn Plantain and English Stonecrop. Maritime grassland covers much of the north-west side and forms a narrow zone behind the southern shore. Thrift and Sea Beet are abundant and the nationally rare Shore Dock has also been recorded. Tree Mallow and Small Reed also occur here.

Vegetation is very limited on the exposed cliffs of Men-a-vaur although there are small pockets of Tree Mallow, Common Scurvygrass and Orache. However, this small rocky islet supports 8 species of breeding seabirds, including the largest colonies in Scilly of Razorbill, Fulmar and Guillemot. Kittiwake and Puffin breed both on Men-a-vaur and on St Helen's and other breeding species include Great Black-backed Gull, Lesser Black-backed Gull, Herring Gull and Shag.

ST MARY'S

Lower Moors

Lower Moors lies east of Hugh Town and consists of a range of wetland habitats on alluvium and peat overlying granite bedrock. Common Reed dominates much of the site, fringed by Grey Willow. Small populations of Royal Fern, Greater Tussock Sedge and Southern Marsh Orchid occur amidst abundant Hemlock Water-dropwort, Lesser Spearwort, Water Mint, Common Marsh- bedstraw and Marsh Pennywort. Soft Rush, Yellow Iris, Ragged Robin and Greater Bird's-foot-trefoil grow in the wet meadows. Small areas of open water are important for passage and wintering Snipe and Water Rail, and Corncrake and Spotted Crake have been recorded on the wet meadows and in the reed beds. The Short-winged Cone-head was found here in 1996. A footpath

St Mary's in the snow
Simon Ford

and boardwalk provide easy access to this site and visitors are encourage to enjoy the nature trail and bird hides at this nature reserve, which is easily accessible from Hugh Town.

Porth Hellick Pool

Porth Hellick Pool is the largest area of open water on St Mary's and is separated from the sea by a vegetated sand and shingle bar, where the dominant plant is Sea Sandwort with occasional Sea Kale. The stream which flows from Holy Vale into the Pool is the only running water of any size on Scilly. Although the Pool is freshwater, some salt-enduring species occur including Sea Club-rush, Saltmarsh Rush, Brackish Water-crowfoot and Sea-milkwort. Most of the Pool is fringed with Common Reed and Grey Willow, with some Bulrush. The surrounding water-logged soils are home to typical wetland species such as Soft Rush, Yellow Iris, Lesser Spearwort, Gypsywort, Water Mint, Hemlock Water-dropwort and Ragged Robin, with small stands of Royal Fern, Greater Tussock Sedge and Southern Marsh Orchid. More acidic boggy areas are revealed by the presence of Bog Pimpernel, Star Sedge, Bog Stitchwort and Bog Pondweed. The Pool and surrounding reed beds are important for breeding birds, including Mallard, Gadwall, Teal, Coot, Moorhen and Sedge Warbler. The site also provides valuable food and shelter for wintering birds and regularly attracts rare vagrant birds.

Peninnis Head

This spectacular headland on the south side of St Mary's supports a range of maritime heathland, maritime grassland and scrub habitats. It is also important because it lies to the south of the glacial limit in the Isles of Scilly and therefore provides an interesting comparison with the glaciated bedrock areas in the north of the islands. The thin soils overlying granite combined with the extreme exposure have lead to the development of wind pruned "waved" maritime heath dominated by Heather, Bell Heather and Western Gorse, although in some areas European Gorse and Bracken scrub is invading and thereby changing the character of the landscape. Species-rich maritime grassland occurs near the cliff edges, with Thrift, Yorkshire Fog, Sorrel, Buck's-horn Plantain, Common Scurvy-grass and Red Fescue. The rare plants Early Meadow-grass and Western Clover have been recorded here. There is a rich lichen flora: *Ramalina siliquosa* occurs extensively, together with the rare *Roccella fucoides* and Golden Hair-lichen.

Peninnis Head

Wall on Samson

SAMSON

Samson is the largest uninhabited island in the Isles of Scilly and is situated on the north-western side of the archipelago. Nearby there are the small islands of Puffin Island, Stony Island, Green Island and White Island.

Samson is just over a kilometre long, from Bollard Point in the north to Southward Well Point in the south, and consists of two granite hills rising to over 40 metres separated by a low narrow neck of vegetated sand and shingle. Thin podzol soils surround the tor-topped hills, whilst the adjacent hill slopes have deeper, well drained soils. Blown sand has formed a small dune system in the north-east corner of the island.

The small areas of lowland acidic heath on the tops of North and South Hill are exposed to severe winds which have produced a dwarf wind-pruned vegetation dominated by Heather, Bell Heather and Western Gorse. The surrounding slopes have a dense Bracken cover together with Bramble, Honeysuckle, Bluebell and Red Campion. There is also a good population of the nationally rare Balm-leaved Figwort and the small spring on South Hill supports Blunt-fruited Water-starwort and Blinks.

The small dune system is dominated by Marram Grass whilst the well-developed strandline vegetation is particularly important for the occurrence of the nationally rare Shore Dock. The spring on

the south east shore has Greater Skullcap, its only known station on Scilly.

The vegetation of Samson also reflects the long period of human occupation of the island prior to the final evacuation in 1855, and introduced plant species (including Tamarisk, Elder and Primrose) occur around the old ruins and walls on the south side of the island.

Samson and the surrounding islands are also of particular note for their seabird colonies, including six species of breeding seabirds. North Hill and Green Island support a nationally important breeding colony of Common Tern, whilst Roseate Tern breed on North Hill and Green Island. There are

Terns nesting signs on Samson

Leaving Samson

also recent records of Sandwich Tern on Green Island. Samson has by far the largest colonies of Lesser Black-backed Gull and Herring Gull in the archipelago. In addition, there is a small breeding colony of Great Black-backed Gull and Shag breed on Puffin Island. In the past many of the breeding seabird colonies, especially the terns, have suffered from rats eating the eggs. However, a recent major rat eradication programme has been undertaken in an attempt to make Samson rat-free.

There are no restrictions on landing on Samson (although there are on Stony Island and Green Island) and it provides visitors with the unique experience of being able to spend time on a deserted, uninhabited island rich in archaeology and wildlife. Only during the bird breeding season are visitors asked to refrain from visiting the fragile and vulnerable tern nesting areas, although these graceful birds can still be seen at very close quarters.

TEAN

Tean is an uninhabited island located 1.5 km to the east of Tresco on the north-east side of the archipelago. It is composed of a series of granite tors, of which Great Hill rises to over 40 metres. In between lies lower land, overlain with glacial till and gravels. Glacial erratics are abundant on the beaches to the north and north west of the island, marking the approximate southern limit of soliflucted outwash gravels on Scilly.

The areas of dune grassland behind East and West Porth are particularly important for the presence of the very rare Dwarf Pansy, a plant which occurs on Scilly and nowhere else in Great Britain. The rare Four-leaved Allseed also occurs on the island and there are several populations of Balm-leaved Figwort. Areas of maritime grassland where Thrift and Sea Campion are abundant and occur on both sides of St Helen's Porth and on the south of the island near to Clodgie Point, where Orange Bird's-foot also grows.

A small area of lowland heath can be found at the summit of Great Hill, but much of the remainder of Tean is dominated by Bracken growing on previously cultivated parts of the island. Human influence on the island is considerable since it was inhabited as long ago as the Bronze Ages and more recently from 1684 to after 1800. About 8 hectares were once walled off and cultivated and these areas still possess relict pasture plants such as Red Clover, Hop Trefoil, Black Knapweed, Rye Grass and Yellow Oat Grass.

The island also supports several breeding seabirds including a small colony of Puffin (on the east side of the island), Lesser Black-backed Gull, Kittiwake, Herring Gull and a few Great Black-backed Gulls. Following a reduction in the Puffin population, artificial burrows have been excavated in the cliffs to try and encourage more Puffins to return and breed in the colony. It is still too soon to judge whether this experimental management will be suceesful.

TRESCO

Appletree Banks and Pentle Bay

These areas comprise an extensive sand dune system (the largest on Scilly) merging into lichen-rich heathland on the eastern side of Tresco. Much of the site is overlain by wind blown sand although granite outcrops in places to form several low-lying carns and offshore islands. The strandline vegetation includes Sea Rocket, together with Sea Purslane and Sea Spurge. The nationally rare Shore Dock occurs in the backshore area. The low dunes behind the beach are dominated by Marram with Sand Sedge, Sea Stork's-bill, Bird's-foot Clover, Suffocated Clover and Portland Spurge. The dunes are particularly important for two nationally rare plants, Balm-leaved Figwort and Babington's Leek, both of which are abundant here. Bramble is a rampant coloniser of the dunes and further inland Bracken has invaded areas of deeper soil.

The hummocky heathland at Appletree Banks is dominated by Heather and Bell Heather with Common Bird's-foot-trefoil and Orange Bird's-foot. This part of Tresco is especially important for its rare lichen flora including several nationally rare oceanic species such as the Ciliate Strap-lichen *Heterodermi leucomelos* and *Pseudocyphellaria aurata*. Here too are to be found the Lungwort lichens, *Lobaria pulmonaria* and *Lobaria scrobiculata*, growing on heather rather than on deciduous trees as on the mainland. Such lichen-rich heathlands are internationally important and there are few similar sites in Europe. Several rare bryophytes also occur here, including the liverworts *Lophocolea semiteres* and *Fossombronia foveolata*. One of the larger colonies of Common Tern on Scilly breed on the heathland and dunes. Common Terns also breed on nearby Merrick Island and some of the other small rocks and islets. In most years Roseate Terns also manage to breed provided that the locations are kept free from disturbance and predation.

Great Pool

This is the largest area of freshwater on Scilly and stretches for 1km across the central part of the island. The Pool is protected from the sea by a narrow sandbank at Abbey Farm to the west and wider sand dunes to the east. Alluvium, silt and peat overlay the granite rock, producing a shallow mesotrophic (i.e. with average nutrient levels) lake. The shallow water at the edges supports the rare Brackish Water-crowfoot, together with Alternate Water-milfoil and Fennel Pondweed. The adjacent marginal vegetation is dominated by dense Common Reed, with Bulrush abundant at the southern end. Spongy waterlogged soils support Royal Fern, Tubular Water-dropwort and Soft Rush. Grey Willow forms a dense border on the northern edge of the wetland, with Yellow Iris and Marsh Pennywort. The drier areas support Stinking Iris, Creeping Buttercup, Lesser Celandine, Balm-leaved Figwort and Babington's Leek.

The Pool and surrounding reed beds and willow carr are important for breeding birds such as Mute Swan, Mallard, Gadwall, Water Rail, Sedge Warbler and Reed Warbler. Overwintering birds include Teal, Wigeon, Shoveler, Mallard, Gadwall, Pochard and Tufted Duck. The site is also a valuable feeding and sheltering area for a large number of passage birds, including vagrants from North America. A boardwalk through the reed beds on the north side of the Pool provides access to the bird hide, which was erected in memory of David Hunt, former Tresco Abbey gardener, local ornithologist and much loved "Birdman of Scilly".

Castle Down

Granite underlies this exposed headland on the north side of Tresco, forming a low windswept pla-teau only 35 metres above sea level. A small cave called Piper's Hole has been hollowed out of the raised-beach deposits in the cliffs on the northeast coast; several troglophiles (species adapted to life in caves) have been recorded here, including at least two species new to Britain. (Access to Piper's Hole is rather precarious and much of the cave is occupied by a narrow lake). 'Waved' maritime heathland covers much of the central part of the Down, with Heather, Bell Heather and Western Gorse. Few other plants occur in this wind-pruned habitat, although Bracken and Bramble scrub grows in the more sheltered areas with deeper soils. Castle Downs is of particular importance for its lichen flora, exhibiting a range of rare oceanic heathland species including the only known European record of Coralloid Rosette-lichen *Heterodermia propagulifera* together with Ciliate Strap-lichen *Heterodermia obscurata*. These *Heterodermia* communities are now very rare and comparable sites, outside Scilly, occur only in Brittany and the Channel Isles. The 45 species of lichen recorded here also include Lungwort growing on Heather and a number of *Cladonia* species which dominate the shallow soils and open pans on the central heathland. This short lichen-rich heathland supports an important breeding colony of Common Tern.

Great Pool, Tresco

WESTERN ROCKS

The Western Rocks lie on the western edge of the archipelago between Annet and Bishop Rock. They comprise a series of small uninhabited granite islands including Great Crebawethan, Rosevear, Rosevean, Gorregan, Melledgan and Hellweathers together with numerous other isolated rocks and ledges. All of the islands are low lying, reaching a maximum height of only 17 metres on Rosevean and hence they are all exposed to the full force of the Atlantic south west gales and excessive salt spray. Shallow skeletal soils are mainly confined to the larger islands; elsewhere soils are only found in isolated pockets in the granite. These thin soils and the extreme exposure severely limit the vegetation and only six species of vascular plant have been recorded. All six species are found on Rosevear where Tree Mallow occurs in abundance, together with Sea Beet, Common Scurvygrass, Rock Sea-spurrey, Orache, and Curled Dock. Some of the other islands and rocks including Great Crebawethan are often completely devoid of flowering plants.

The Western Rocks are of particular importance as a seabird colony supporting 11 species of breeding seabirds. The breeding colony of Shag is of national importance; it is also the largest colony of this species in the archipelago, with the colony on Rosevear being of particular note. The island of Gorregan has breeding colonies of Kittiwake, Razorbill and Guillemot. Cormorant breed on Melledgan and Storm Petrel breed on some of the granite boulder beaches throughout these western islands. The other breeding seabirds include Puffin, Fulmar, Great Black-backed Gull, Lesser Black-backed Gull and Herring Gull.

In addition, the isolated rocks and islands of the Western Rocks provide the most important breeding site on Scilly for Grey Seal, which can often be seen hauled-out at low water on Grear and Little Crebawethan or Wee Rock. A boat trip around Annet and out to the Western Rocks, especially in the bird breeding season, is the highlight of any visit to Scilly. Visitors are advised to take this trip as soon as the weather allows the tripper boats to venture out to the western extremities of the archipelago, sometimes as far as the Bishop Rock Lighthouse. It is an unforgettable wildlife experience.

Rosevear

WHITE ISLAND

This small uninhabited island is located off the north side of St Martin's. Thin skeletal soils and extreme exposure have lead to the development of wind pruned "waved" maritime heath dominated by Heather, Bell Heather and Western Gorse, together with Common Bird's-foot-trefoil, Heath Bedstraw and English Stonecrop. The more sheltered areas with deeper soils have Bracken, Bramble and Honeysuckle. Small areas of short-turfed maritime grassland occur along the western coastal margin, where Thrift, Sea Beet, Red Fescue, Common Scurvygrass and Buck's-horn Plantain are common. Lesser Black-backed Gull, Herring Gull, Great Black-backed Gull, Kittiwake and Fulmar nest in the more isolated habitats.

St Martin's from the air

USEFULL ADDRESSES

Cornwall and Isles of Scilly Federation of Biological Recorders, Tremayne Farm Cottage, Praze-an-Beeble, Camborne, Cornwall TR14 9PH.

English Nature, Trevint House, Stangways Villas, Truro, Cornwall TR1 2PA.

Isles of Scilly Environmental Trust, The Parade, St Mary's.

PHOTOGRAPHS

All photographs in this book are by the authors, Pat Sargeant and Adrian Spalding except where indicated.
Pat Sargeant: photographs on pages 1, 5, 6, 8, 10, 17, 18, 20, 22, 23, 25, 28, 29, 30, 32, 33, 34, 36, 38, 39, 41, 42, 43, 45 and 46
Adrian Spalding: photographs on pages 3, 4, 6, 9, 11, 12, 14, 15, 16, 24, 35, 37 and 39

SELECT BIBLIOGRAPHY

Agassiz, D.   *A Revised List of the Lepidoptera of the Isles of Scilly.* Isles of Scilly Museum Association. St Mary's. 1981.

Blair, K.G.   The beetles of the Scilly Islands. *Proceedings of the Zoological Society.* 4: 1211-1258. 1931.

Gibson, F.   *Wild Flowers of Scilly.* (no date)

Gibson, F. & Murrish, P. (Eds).   *A Precious Heritage.* Isles of Scilly Environmental Trust. St Mary's. 1990.

Groves, M.   *Exploring Underwater. The Isles of Scilly.* Porth Books. St Agnes (Cornwall). 1988.

Hale, J. & Hicks, M.   Lepidoptera of St Agnes, Isles of Scilly. Springtime 1997, early or late? *Atropos.* 4: 29-32. 1998.

Hiscock, K.   *Sublittoral Survey of the Isles of Scilly.* Field Studies Council. 1983.

Hyatt, K.H.   The Acarine Fauna of the Isles of Scilly. *Cornish Studies, Second Series.* 1:120-161. 1993.

Lousley, J.E.   *The Flora of the Isles of Scilly.* David & Charles. Newton Abbot. 1971.

Lousley, J.E.   (Revised by Clare Harvey, 1983). *Flowering Plants and Ferns in the Isles of Scilly.* Isles of Scilly Museum Association. St Mary's. 1975.

Penhallurick. R.D.   *Turtles off Cornwall, The Isles of Scilly and Devonshire.* Dyllansow Pengwella. Truro. 1990.

Penhallurick. R.D.   *The Butterflies of Cornwall and the Isles of Scilly.* Dyllansow Pengwella. Truro. 1996.

Ratcliffe J. & Straker, V.   *The Early Environment of Scilly.* Cornwall Archaeological Unit, Cornwall County Council. Truro. 1996.

Spalding, A.   *Cornwall's Butterfly & Moth Heritage.* Twelveheads Press, Truro, 1992

Spalding, A. (Ed.).   *Red Data Book for Cornwall and the Isles of Scilly.* Croceago Press. Praze-an-Beeble. 1997.

Smith, F.H.N.   *The moths and butterflies of Cornwall and the Isles of Scilly.* Gem Publishing. Wallingford. 1997.

Wagstaff, W.   *Isles of Scilly Bird Checklist.* Isles of Scilly Environmental Trust. St Mary's. 1995.

Pulpit rock   Beth Tonkin

ISBN 0906294 44 4   © Adrian Spalding and Pat Sargeant, 2000
First published 2000 by Twelveheads Press, Chy Mengleth, Twelveheds, Truro, Cornwall TR4 8SN